W9-CAV-202

"The expectation level is high at the University of Alabama and it should be. What's wrong with people expecting excellence?"

–Gene Stallings

STEWART, TABORI & CHANG
NEW YORK

RON GREEN, JR.

101 REASONS TO LOVE
ALABAMA
★ FOOTBALL ★

INTRODUCTION

If you've lived in the South, you understand how much tradition is a part of life there. There are ties to the past that bond families to one another, their friends, their churches, their towns, even as life rolls forward. When it comes to allegiances, particularly in college football, the South holds fast to what is close to the heart.

Nowhere is that more evident than with Alabama football. To say it is a football program doesn't do it justice. Alabama football is both a way of life and a state of being. The games may be played in the fall, but the passion for the sport lives year-round.

Taylor Zarzour is like thousands born and raised with Crimson Tide football.

"My first memories in life are of watching Alabama football," says Zarzour, who was born in Mobile into a family full of Alabama alums.

Zarzour, now a sports talk radio host in the Raleigh-Durham (N.C.) area, remembers meeting Bear Bryant as a child. The way Zarzour remembers it, Bryant told the youngster he would take him fishing one day, and within two weeks, Bryant was gone. Others in the family remember the details a bit differently, though the essence of the moment is genuine.

As if Zarzour didn't already know the spirit surrounding Alabama football, it was reinforced on the afternoon of October 28, 1989. When Alabama's Thomas Rayam blocked what would have been a game-winning field goal to secure a 17–16 victory at Penn State, Zarzour saw his mother, Katherine, jump excitedly onto a coffee table. She was 8 ½ months pregnant at the time.

That is the passion of Alabama football. It explains why the spring football game—A-Day at Alabama—can draw more than 70,000 fans.

Alabama football is Bear Bryant and Big Al, Don Hutson and Joe Namath, "the Run in the Mud," and the "Goal-Line Stand." It's Bryant-Denny Stadium, tailgating at the Quad, and "Rammer Jammer Yellow Hammer." It's a houndstooth hat, the third Saturday in October, and eight consensus national championships.

It's a tradition.

1 MAMA CALLED

In 1957, Paul "Bear" Bryant was the head football coach at Texas A&M, until he was approached by Alabama officials about returning to his alma mater to become football coach and athletic director.

"I left Texas A&M because my school called me," Bryant said. "Mama called, and when Mama calls, then you just have to come running."

To Bryant and many thousands more, Alabama football is the tie that binds.

Bear Bryant

2 W. G. LITTLE

Though not the most famous name in Alabama's rich football history, William G. Little may be the most important because he is credited with bringing the game to Tuscaloosa. Little discovered the game while attending Phillips Exeter Academy in New Hampshire. He returned to Alabama after his brother's death and enrolled in the university in 1892. That fall, Little taught the game to some fellow students, and the rest, as they say, is history.

3 THE FIRST GAME

The glory days of Southeastern Conference (SEC) football were still years away when Alabama played its first official game on November 11, 1892. Playing at Lakeview Park in Birmingham, the first team, with Little as captain, faced a team of players pulled from Birmingham high schools and a private school. E. B. Beaumont owns the distinction of being Alabama's first football coach. It was a beautiful beginning, as Alabama won, 56–0.

4 THE FANS

For legions, young and old, Alabama football is a way of life. It's passed down from generation to generation, families and friendships tied by their connection to a football program that is based in Tuscaloosa but reaches across the nation. Sellouts long ago became routine at Bryant-Denny Stadium, where game days are like holidays. For Tide fans, it's about the past, the present, and the future. It's about still being able to see Bear Bryant leaning on a goalpost, Van Tiffin beating Auburn, and a stroll around Denny Chimes, where the names of the past stay alive. It's about tailgating and cheerleading and living for those special Saturdays. It's about Alabama football.

Bully Vandergraaff attempts to
make a diving tackle, circa 1915.

5 WHEN FOOTBALL ENDED

It didn't take long for the game to become popular among Alabama students and others. However, the university administration didn't have the same early affection for football. In 1896, the university's board of trustees passed a rule forbidding the school's athletic teams from playing games away from the campus. Alabama played just one football game in 1897 and disbanded the program the following season. But the popularity of the new sport, particularly among the students, led the trustees to reconsider their position. They lifted the ban on off-campus competition, and the sport was renewed in 1899.

6 THE QUAD

It's been nearly 100 years since Alabama quit playing football games on the Quad, but that remains the spot where the football experience comes alive in Tuscaloosa. It's where Saturdays become a celebration of the Crimson Tide. It's where stories are told, acquaintances are renewed, lunches are shared, little girls wear Alabama cheerleading outfits, footballs are tossed, and memories are made. It's where the program's legends congregate to sign autographs and where the band begins its "Elephant Stomp to Bryant-Denny Stadium." It's where Alabama began playing home games in 1893 and where it lives on each autumn.

7 THE THIN RED LINE

This was the original nickname of Alabama's football team. It was obviously tied to the school's crimson color and was adopted by newspapers in the area. It lasted until 1907, when a rainstorm changed the nickname forever.

8 THE CRIMSON TIDE

It was 1907 when the famous nickname was born. Alabama and Auburn were playing in Birmingham, and the weather was miserable. Although Auburn was a solid favorite to win, Alabama managed a 6–6 tie in muddy conditions. Hugh Roberts, sports editor of the *Birmingham Age-Herald*, is credited with originating the Crimson Tide name. Other writers latched onto it, and soon it became the school's official athletic nickname. Interestingly, the Alabama-Auburn game in 1907 was the last meeting between the rival schools for 41 years.

9 THE CAPSTONE

In 1913, university president G. H. Denny (whose name is currently on the football stadium) proclaimed the school to be "the capstone of the public school system in the state." Soon, friends and alums were calling the university "the Capstone," and anyone who has attended Alabama is familiar with the Capstone Creed. It reads: "As a member of the University of Alabama community, I will pursue knowledge; act with fairness, honesty and respect; foster civic responsibility; and strive for excellence."

Alabama versus Georgia, 1925

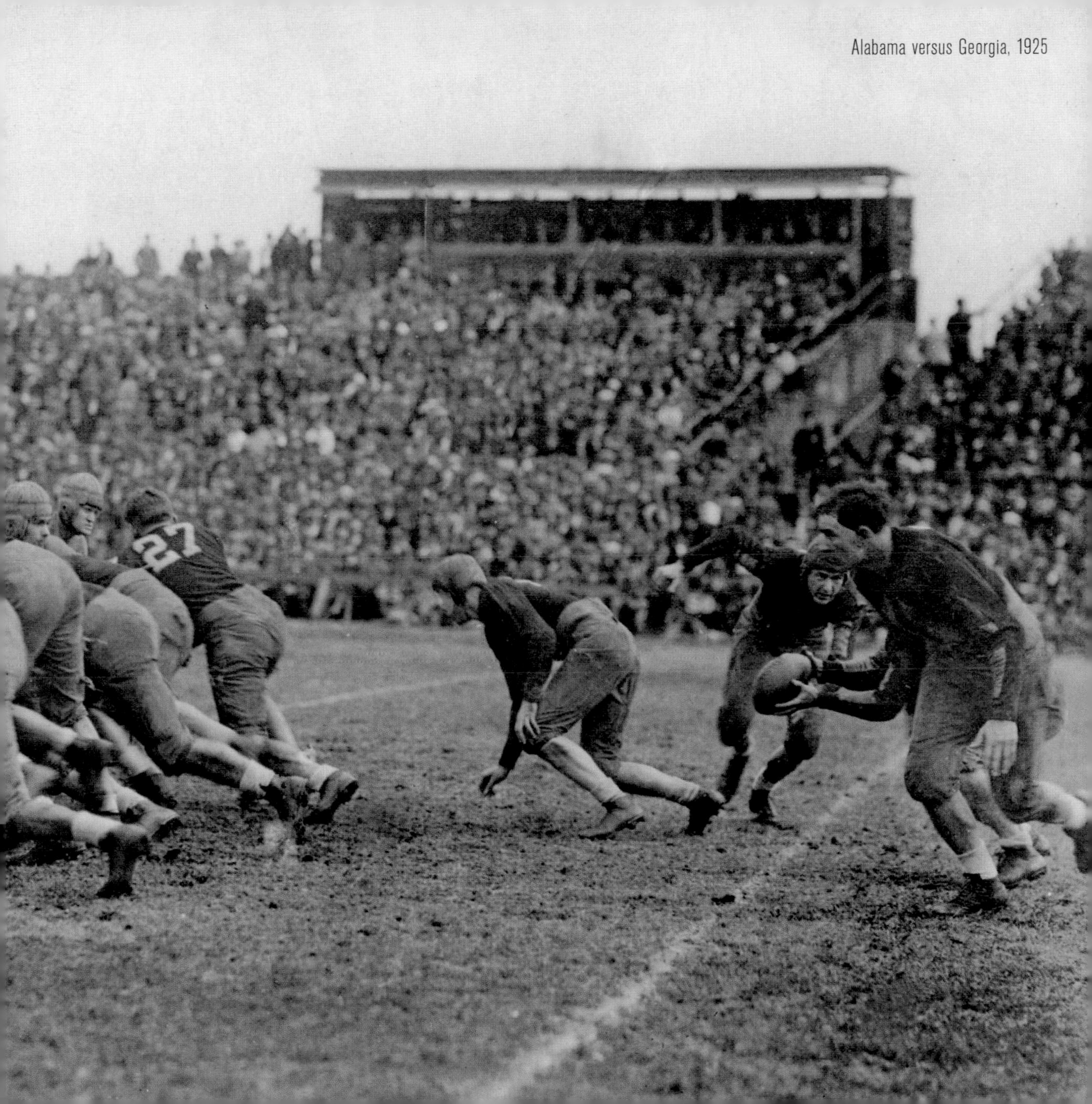

Glen Coffee versus Florida, 2008

10 THE BIRTH OF THE SEC

In 1921, Alabama joined 13 other schools in forming the Southern Conference. Over the next few years, the league expanded to 23 teams, covering a vast territory from Florida to Maryland to Louisiana. In 1933, 13 of the schools—including Alabama—pulled away to form the Southeastern Conference. Alabama wasted no time establishing its football superiority, winning the league's first championship in 1933.

11 SEC FOOTBALL

It is the epitome of college football, not just for the games but for the passion and the experience. It's Saturday at the Grove in Oxford, Mississippi; the orange-and-white checkerboard end zones at Tennessee's Neyland Stadium; Uga, the Georgia mascot; the Swamp in Gainesville, Florida; the Third Saturday in October; and the *2001: A Space Odyssey* theme playing at South Carolina. It's where Archie Manning, Herschel Walker, Don Hutson, Lee Roy Jordan, Jake Scott, and Charlie Trippi played. It's the first conference to hold its own championship game, and it's a fixture on television sets across the country on Saturday afternoons and evenings throughout the fall. It's like nothing else.

Pooley Hubert scores versus Washington in the 1926 Rose Bowl.
Inset: Wallace Wade

12 WALLACE WADE

Wade is one of the legendary names in college coaching, largely because of the eight seasons he spent at Alabama, cultivating a program that would come to define southern football. Known as a disciplinarian, Wade quickly established Alabama as a national power known for playing smothering defense. His 1930 team shut out eight of the 10 opponents it faced, including Washington State in the 1931 Rose Bowl—using just the second-stringers. After the 1930 season, Wade startled college football by leaving Alabama for Duke. Wade left behind a record of 61–13–3 and three national championships.

13 ALABAMA AND THE ROSE BOWL

For a time, Alabama made Pasadena, California, feel almost like a second home. The Tide became the first team from the South to play in the Rose Bowl when it went west in 1926 and beat favored Washington, 20–19, to cap an unbeaten 1925 season and claim the school's first national championship. In 1927, Alabama returned to the Rose Bowl, where it played Stanford—coached by Pop Warner—to a 7–7 tie and claimed a second national championship. Wallace Wade's final Alabama team wrapped up a third national championship with a 24–0 win over Washington State in 1931. The Tide would make three more trips to Pasadena, in 1935, 1938, and 1946, before bowl officials decided to make the game an annual matchup of teams from the Pac-10 Conference and the Big Ten.

1926 Rose Bowl
Inset: Johnny Mack Brown

14 JOHNNY MACK BROWN

Brown was called "the Dothan Antelope," a nod to his hometown and his spectacular skills on the football field. It was Brown who played the starring role in Alabama's 1925 national championship story, including a two-touchdown performance in the Tide's upset victory over Washington in the 1926 Rose Bowl, which earned him a Most Valuable Player award. Brown eventually was inducted into the College Football Hall of Fame, but he was more than a football player. The former Alabama halfback became a movie star, appearing in more than 160 films during his career, most of them westerns. He has a star honoring him on the Hollywood Walk of Fame.

15 POOLEY HUBERT

He was one of the early stars of Alabama football, teaming with Johnny Mack Brown to play a key role in the 1925 national championship season. Hubert arrived at Alabama as a 21-year-old freshman after military service, and by the time he was a senior, his teammates were calling him "Papa Pooley." He played quarterback and fullback on offense, but was at his best as a defensive back. That's where Pooley had a huge impact in sealing the Tide's 20–19 Rose Bowl victory over Washington. He was inducted into the College Football Hall of Fame in 1964.

16 FRED SINGTON

Sington is a member of the College Football Hall of Fame, but labeling him a football player doesn't do justice to everything he was. He played tackle for Alabama from 1928 through 1930, when Wallace Wade was the Crimson Tide coach. As a senior, Sington was named an All-American. In addition, he was Phi Beta Kappa, president of the student body as a senior, and a member of the baseball, basketball, and track teams at Alabama. He played professional baseball and rose to the rank of lieutenant commander during World War II. Eventually, Sington ended up back in Alabama, where he was chairman of the first Hall of Fame Bowl, played in Birmingham in 1977.

Pooley Hubert breaks into the open field versus Washington in the 1926 Rose Bowl. Inset: Fred Sington

17 FRANK THOMAS

Although he had the difficult task of succeeding Wallace Wade, Thomas created his own legacy during 15 years as the Alabama football coach (1931–46, with no games in 1943). Thomas had been the starting quarterback for three seasons at Notre Dame, where he played for Coach Knute Rockne. While at Notre Dame, Thomas was the roommate of George "the Gipper" Gipp. As a coach at Alabama, Thomas had a 115–24–7 record, which included national championships in 1934 and 1941. His teams were characterized by outstanding defense: During Thomas' 15 years at Alabama, opponents averaged just 6.3 points per game against the Tide. While at Alabama, Thomas coached a number of exceptional players, including Don Hutson and Paul "Bear" Bryant. Thomas' place in Alabama history is memorialized by his statue, which stands outside Bryant-Denny Stadium.

18 FRANK HOWARD

He was called "the Baron of Barlow Bend," a reference to the tiny town he called home. And eventually, Frank Howard was also called a member of the College Football Hall of Fame. Howard learned football at Alabama, where he played along the offensive line for three years starting in 1928, despite weighing less than 200 pounds. His fame came later at Clemson, where Howard followed Jess Neely, who had been one of his coaches at Alabama. When Neely left Clemson, Howard became head coach there in 1940, a job he kept until he retired after the 1969 season, with a record of 165–118–12.

Big Al and fans

19 THE ELEPHANT MASCOT

At first glance, it's a curious thing—Alabama football having an elephant as its mascot. But there's a story behind it. During Alabama's great 1930 season, when the team posted eight shutouts during a 10–0 season, Everett Strupper wrote a story for the *Atlanta Journal* about the Tide's 64–0 victory over Mississippi in October. Strupper was one of the officials in the game, and he wrote a weekly column about the game he had worked the previous Saturday. He wrote about how Coach Wallace Wade started his second team against Ole Miss. When the second quarter begin, Wade inserted the starters.

Here's what Strupper wrote: "At the end of the quarter, the earth started to tremble, there was a distant rumble that continued to grow. Some excited fan in the stands bellowed, 'Hold your horses, the elephants are coming,' and out stamped the Alabama varsity."

For the rest of the season, writers and fans referred to the Alabama line as the "Red Elephants," and a mascot was born.

20 BIG AL

Although Alabama's football team was called the Red Elephants in 1930, it wasn't until 50 years later that the school created Big Al, a walking, talking, cheerleading elephant. There is some debate as to when Big Al made his debut. Some contend Big Al's first appearance was the 1979 Sugar Bowl, when Alabama played Penn State for the national championship. The Tide beat Penn State, 14–7, that night and claimed another championship. Others say Big Al was introduced one year later at the Sugar Bowl against Arkansas. Regardless, he has become an instantly recognizable aspect of the football program and part of what makes it special.

21 DIXIE HOWELL

In the literary masterpiece *To Kill A Mockingbird*, Scout tries to cheer up her brother by telling him he reminds her of Alabama's Dixie Howell. It was quite a compliment. Howell was one of the early and enduring stars of Alabama football, throwing passes to Don Hutson to create one of the college game's great tandems in the 1930s. His arm earned Howell the nickname "the Human Howitzer."

In the Crimson Tide's 1935 Rose Bowl victory over Stanford, Howell accounted for 313 yards, and he did it in dramatic fashion. He scored on a 5-yard touchdown run in which he somersaulted into the end zone. He also had a 67-yard touchdown run and a scoring pass to Hutson. It was one of five completions Howell had to Hutson that day. He also completed two passes to Alabama's "other end," Bear Bryant.

"He could do it all."

–Kay Francis on Dixie Howell, from *Legends of Alabama Football*

Dixie Howell scores from the 5-yard line in the 1935 Rose Bowl versus Stanford.

Don Hutson prior to
the 1935 Rose Bowl

22 DON HUTSON

When the subject turns to the players who had the greatest impact not just on teams and programs but on the game itself, Don Hutson's name makes the list. But his impact was slow to be felt at Alabama. Until his last season, Hutson was not a prominent player for the Tide. But as a senior, he became an All-American and closed his career with a great day in a Rose Bowl victory. Playing with quarterback Dixie Howell, Hutson kept improving as his senior season unfolded, including a three-touchdown day in a 40–0 win over Clemson. In his final Alabama game, Hutson almost single-handedly destroyed Stanford, catching six passes for 165 yards in a 29–13 victory.

23 HUTSON'S LEGACY

When Don Hutson signed with the Green Bay Packers in 1935, football was a different game, built primarily on the ability to run the ball. Hutson, however, transformed the game, creating many of the pass routes that have become so familiar in modern-day football. A member of three NFL championship teams, Hutson made All-Pro nine times and led the league in receiving eight times. When he retired with 99 touchdown catches, Hutson was 62 ahead of second place. Not only was he a great offensive player, Hutson also scored 193 career points as a place-kicker and intercepted 30 passes as a defensive back. It was as a receiver, though, that Hutson was a pioneer.

"All Hutson can do is beat you."

—Georgia Tech coach Bill Alexander

31

Don Whitmire

24 YEA ALABAMA

What's great football without a great sound track? For Crimson Tide fans, "Yea Alabama" owns a place in their hearts.

Yea, Alabama! Drown 'em Tide!
Every 'Bama man's behind you,
Hit your stride.
Go teach the Bulldogs to behave,
Send the Yellow Jackets to a watery grave.
And if a man starts to weaken,
That's a shame!
For 'Bama's pluck and grit have
Writ her name in Crimson flame.
Fight on, fight on, fight on men!
Remember the Rose Bowl, we'll win then.
So roll on to victory.
Hit your stride,
You're Dixie's football pride,
Crimson Tide, Roll Tide, Roll Tide!

25 DON WHITMIRE

He spent two years as an offensive tackle for the Crimson Tide in 1941–42 before moving to the United States Naval Academy for two seasons. Whitmire was an All-American at Alabama in 1942, then a two-time All-American at Navy. After football, Whitmire rose to the rank of rear admiral in the Navy; during the Vietnam War, he was the man in charge of the evacuation of Saigon in 1975.

Harry Gilmer, Frank Thomas, and Vaughn Mancha at a train station en route to the 1946 Rose Bowl game

26 HARRY GILMER

A native of Birmingham, Gilmer had an enormous impact on the program, which posted a 30–9–2 record during his days in Tuscaloosa, from 1944 to 1947. Gilmer played halfback and defensive back and was known for throwing jump passes, a technique he developed as a child. As a freshman, Gilmer completed all eight passes he threw in a Sugar Bowl victory over Duke. As a sophomore, Gilmer led the nation in touchdown passes (13) and ranked second in total offense (1,457 yards). As a junior, he led the nation in punt return average (14.5). After college, Gilmer played nine years in the NFL and coached another 27 years in the league, then spent 11 seasons as a scout.

27 LEGION FIELD

For years, it was Alabama's home away from home. Located in Birmingham, which was easier for many people to reach than Tuscaloosa, Legion Field once hosted at least three of Alabama's home games each season. Built in 1926, the stadium has been used for a variety of events, including being the host site for the 1996 Olympic Games soccer competition. It has hosted bowl games, concerts, and professional football, but its history is most closely tied to the days when Alabama called it home. From 1948 through 1988, the annual Alabama-Auburn game was played in Legion Field. Gradually, though, the games moved away from Birmingham after the expansion of Bryant-Denny Stadium. Alabama's final home game in Legion Field was played August 30, 2003, against South Florida.

28 THE IRON BOWL

Sports are filled with spirited, colorful, and often bitter rivalries, but there are few, if any, that can rival what happens when Alabama and Auburn play football in late November each year. It divides a state, consumes a region, and, many times, has a direct impact on college football's national championship. Since its inception in 1893, the Alabama-Auburn game has been colored by controversy. It got so bad it was suspended after the 1907 game and not renewed until 1948. For years, it was played at Legion Field in Birmingham, a supposedly neutral site, though both sides took exception to that. It is now played in even years at Alabama's Bryant-Denny Stadium and in odd-numbered years at Auburn's Jordan-Hare Stadium. And it's always played with an uncommon passion that prompted *Sports Illustrated* magazine to name it the second-biggest rivalry in sports, behind only the New York Yankees–Boston Red Sox feud.

"It's the kind of game I didn't enjoy playing in. The game is never over. You keep repeating it and repeating it and repeating it…. It's never over until you play it again next year."

–Mike DuBose, from *A War in Dixie*

Auburn's David Irons attempts to break up a pass intended for Alabama's Will Oakley (7).

29 BRYANT-DENNY STADIUM

The address is 100 Bryant Drive, Tuscaloosa, Alabama, but everyone who knows Alabama football knows where it is. Since 1929, the Crimson Tide has played football at what is now called Bryant-Denny Stadium, though it was not always the team's primary facility. For years, that distinction belonged to Legion Field in Birmingham. Through the years, however, Bryant-Denny Stadium has been expanded and enhanced, and it is now the only home of Alabama football. It began as a 12,000-seat arena named for school president George Denny. In 1975, Bear Bryant's name was attached to it. The stadium now seats 92,138 fans, has 123 skyboxes, and provides innumerable memories, made better by the fact that Alabama has a 210–43–3 record in the building it calls home.

30 THE WALK OF FAME

Since 1948, Alabama football has honored its former captains by having them place their handprints and footprints in cement at the base of Denny Chimes, one of the most recognizable landmarks on campus. The Chimes were built in 1929 to honor former school president George Denny, and the tower reaches 115 feet into the air. It's at ground level, though, that the players who have had an enormous impact on Alabama football are uniquely honored.

31 THE MILLION DOLLAR BAND

At Alabama, it is not just a marching band. It is a vital, proud, spectacular part of the football experience. If Bryant-Denny Stadium is the stage for Alabama football, the Million Dollar Band provides the sound track. As for its name, the story goes that the band had scraped together enough money to travel to Atlanta for a game with Georgia Tech in 1922. The Crimson Tide lost badly that day, and an Atlanta sportswriter said to Alabama booster Champ Pickens, "You don't have much of a team. What do you have at Alabama?" To which Pickens is said to have replied, "A million-dollar band."

32 THE FACILITIES

College football doesn't just happen on Saturdays. It's a year-round endeavor—part of the overall college experience for the players. At Alabama, the commitment to excellence is obvious everywhere. The Bryant Academic Center for student-athletes is filled with computer labs, study halls, classrooms, and lecture halls. There are on-campus apartments for the players, who can dine in the Bryant Grille, a sports-themed dining area that features flat-screen television. The football locker room incorporates the same kind of air-purifying system used by NASA, and the weight room spans 22,000 square feet.

33

BART STARR

In 1955, Alabama went 0–10 with a quarterback who was virtually unnoticed. But the Green Bay Packers saw something in Bart Starr that convinced them to use a 17th-round draft pick on him. It took a while for Starr's talent to show, but when it did, the landscape of professional football changed. Starr is the only starting quarterback to win five NFL championships, and he has the distinction of being named Most Valuable Player in the first two Super Bowls ever played.

"If you work harder than somebody else, chances are you'll beat him though he has more talent than you."

—Bart Starr

"I'll put you through hell, but at the end of it all we'll be champions."
—Bear Bryant

Inset: Bryant celebrating his 314th career win, tying Alonzo Stagg's all-time record, on November 14, 1981

34 BEAR BRYANT

He was and is the essence of Alabama football. Born in Moro Bottom, Arkansas, on September 11, 1913, Bryant grew to become one of the transcendent figures in American sports. He played football at Alabama for four seasons, but he was a football coach in the truest sense of the term. With his deep southern drawl and firm convictions, Bryant came to represent more than a football program. He coached 25 seasons at Alabama (following stops at Maryland, Kentucky, and Texas A&M), and in that time his teams won 13 Southeastern Conference titles and six national championships. When Bryant retired, he was college football's all-time winningest coach, with a cumulative record of 323–85–17 (232–46–9 at Alabama). Bryant was inducted into the College Football Hall of Fame in 1986.

35 THE OTHER END

Although he is known for his coaching success, Bryant also played football at Alabama. He was never a great player, but he was known for his toughness, at one point playing against Tennessee with a partially broken leg. In Alabama's 1934 national championship season, Bryant played end for the Crimson Tide and called himself "the other end," a reference to the fact that the great Don Hutson played on the opposite end.

36 THE NICKNAME

When he was 13 years old, Paul Bryant was told about a traveling promoter coming through Arkansas who was offering $1 to anyone who would wrestle a bear. Bryant went to the Lyric Theater in Fordyce, Arkansas, and got in the ring with the muzzle-wearing bear. When the match began, the bear's muzzle came loose and the bear bit Bryant's ear. Bryant left the theater and never got paid. He did, however, gain a nickname that stuck and became uniquely his.

37 IN THE BEAR'S WORDS

"You must learn how to hold a team together. You must lift some men up, calm others down, until finally they've got one heartbeat. Then you've got yourself a team."

"If wanting to win is a fault, as some of my critics seem to insist, then I plead guilty. I like to win. I know no other way. It's in my blood."

"It's awfully important to win with humility. It's also important to lose. I hate to lose worse than anyone, but if you never lose, you won't know how to act. If you lose with humility, then you can come back."

"*Mama wanted me to be a preacher. I told her coachin' and preachin' were a lot alike.*"

–Bear Bryant

Bear Bryant (12)
and Don Hutson

38 THE HOUNDSTOOTH HAT

If Bear Bryant symbolized Alabama, a houndstooth hat came to symbolize the coach. Bryant began wearing the hat after the 1965 season, and it soon became a part of his image. He received his first hat from former New York Jets owner Sonny Werblin, who tried to hire Bryant to coach his team. Bryant declined the offer but developed a friendship with Werblin, who sent him houndstooth hats regularly through the years.

39 THE PHONE CALL

The story goes that it was early morning when Bear Bryant decided to call his colleague Shug Jordan, the head coach at rival Auburn. Inasmuch as they coached on opposite sides of a state's civil war, they didn't spend much time chatting on the phone. Since it was early morning when Bryant called Jordan, the phone call was answered by a woman, who told the Alabama coach that Jordan wasn't yet at work. "Hell, honey," Bryant is said to have responded, "is anybody down there serious about football?"

"It's not the will to win, but the will to prepare to win that makes the difference."

—Bear Bryant

Dreamland Bar-B-Que

40 BREAKFAST AT THE WAYSIDER

The red-and-white restaurant at 1512 Greensboro Avenue in Tuscaloosa has 16 tables and a place of honor among Alabama football fans. It's where you can get eggs, grits, country ham and red-eye gravy, and the kids can eat pancakes. It's a place where the biscuits are fluffy delicacies and where Crimson Tide football is always on the menu.

41 DREAMLAND BAR-B-QUE

It is the taste of Alabama football. And is it any coincidence that "Big Daddy" John Bishop opened the original Dreamland in 1958, the same year Bear Bryant became head coach in Tuscaloosa? Dreamland, which now has a handful of locations throughout the South, is about barbecue, sauce, and white bread: simple, straightforward, and classic. Using a hickory-fired brick pit to cook pork ribs, Dreamland has become a cultural touchstone around Tuscaloosa and beyond. It's the barbecue served in Bryant-Denny Stadium and a facet of the Alabama football tradition.

42 THE HOUNDSTOOTH SPORTS BAR

Since 1988, the Houndstooth has been a part of the Alabama football experience. Located at 1300 University Boulevard, the Houndstooth is more than a place to grab a burger or a cold beer. It's a place where Alabama football lives. Stuffed with Alabama memorabilia and Crimson Tide fans, the Houndstooth features more than 40 high-definition televisions, a view of Bryant-Denny Stadium, and thousands of stories. A recent renovation gave the Houndstooth a new foundation, but it kept the familiar feel, and for good reason. The Houndstooth has been voted the top college sports bar in the United States by *Sports Illustrated* magazine and was ranked 14th among all sports bars.

"No matter why you are in Dreamland, you will be treated as kin."

–Dreamlandbbq.com

Billy Neighbors (73, far left) upends Lance
Alworth of Arkansas in the 1962 Sugar Bowl.

43 DIGGER O'DELL'S FIELD GOAL

Little had gone right for the Crimson Tide in their 1960 matchup with Georgia Tech—the Yellowjackets led 15–0 at halftime. Coach Bear Bryant took the blame for not having his team ready, but when the final minute arrived, the Tide had the ball trailing 15–13. With 14 seconds remaining, Alabama ran a pass play that moved the ball to the Georgia Tech 12, and the Tide called time out with three seconds remaining. That's when Bryant turned to backup kicker Richard "Digger" O'Dell and asked him to kick the winning field goal. O'Dell had never attempted a field goal in a game.

"Hell, son, it's a piece of cake," Bryant is quoted as saying in *The Bear*, by Don Keith. "Just take a deep breath and put your toe into it . . . just like you do in practice."

That's what O'Dell did, and he was the unlikely hero of a 16–15 victory. It was the only field goal of O'Dell's Alabama career.

44 BILLY NEIGHBORS

According to the College Football Hall of Fame, Neighbors was one of 108 freshman football players who arrived at Alabama in 1958, and he heard Coach Bear Bryant promise a national championship to anyone who stuck it out for four years. Neighbors was one of nine members of that freshman class who stayed the four years, and his play at defensive tackle was one of the reasons the Tide won the 1961 national championship. With Neighbors anchoring the line and Lee Roy Jordan at linebacker, the Tide allowed only 25 points that season and earned a place in history.

"*Lee Roy was the best college linebacker—bar none. He would have made every tackle on every play if they had stayed in bounds.*"

–Bear Bryant on Lee Roy Jordan

Lee Roy Jordan (54) taking aim at
Oklahoma's Jim Grisham (45) in
the 1963 Orange Bowl

45 LEE ROY JORDAN

Jordan was a powerful force at linebacker during his three seasons at Alabama, and he would remain a force in the NFL. Jordan played a central role in the Crimson Tide's 11–0 national championship season in 1961, and he was a first-team All-American as a senior, when the Tide won 10 of 11 games. He closed his college career by making 30 tackles in a 17–0 victory over Oklahoma in the Orange Bowl. Jordan later became a part of the Dallas Cowboys' famous "Doomsday Defense."

46 THE 1961 TEAM

When the discussion turns to college football's greatest teams, Alabama's 1961 squad is among the first to be mentioned. Although it was the school's sixth national championship, it was the first under Coach Bear Bryant, and it signaled a new day in Crimson Tide football. In a word, the '61 team was overwhelming. The Crimson Tide went 11–0 behind quarterback Pat Trammell, center/linebacker Lee Roy Jordan, and offensive lineman Billy Neighbors. Perhaps most impressive was how utterly dominant Alabama was that season, outscoring its opposition 297–25. The Tide posted six shutouts and never allowed more than seven points in a game, eventually capping its national title run with a 10–3 Sugar Bowl win over Arkansas.

47 JOE NAMATH

It would seem, on the surface, that Namath's playboy image was in stark contrast to what Alabama coach Bear Bryant wanted in his program. And there were times when they tangled, as evidenced in Namath's two-game suspension at the end of the 1963 season. But Namath and Bryant had a special relationship. How special? Bryant called Namath "the greatest athlete I ever coached." Namath was exceptional. He had a career record of 29–4 at Alabama and led the Tide to the 1964 national championship.

"When you have confidence, you can have a lot of fun. And when you have fun, you can do amazing things."

–Joe Namath

Joe Namath looks at an open receiver against the University of Texas, 1965 Orange Bowl.

"*There is no way to describe the pride an Alabama player feels in himself and the tradition of the school.*"

–Ken Stabler

Ken Stabler (12) prepares to pass versus Nebraska, 1967 Sugar Bowl.

48 KEN STABLER

Although he grew into a great character during his sparkling NFL career with the Oakland Raiders, Stabler's talent as a quarterback began shining through during his days at Alabama. As a freshman, the left-hander watched as Joe Namath led the Crimson Tide to the 1964 national championship. A year later, Stabler and Steve Sloan shared the quarterback duties and led Alabama to another national championship. Stabler didn't often lose in his college career. He led the Tide to an 11–0 season in 1966, but Alabama wasn't awarded the national championship. In his senior year, the Tide went 8–2–1, but Stabler's place in the program's history was already secure.

49 THE RUN IN THE MUD

By Alabama standards at the time, the Tide's 8–2–1 record in 1967 wasn't anything special, especially after two national championships and one 11–0 season in the previous three years. But senior quarterback Ken Stabler provided the season's most memorable moment in the Iron Bowl show against Auburn. On a wet, dreary day that produced a sloppy game, Auburn was leading Alabama 3–0 late in the game when Stabler changed everything. Rumbling around the right side, Stabler ran 53 yards for the game's only touchdown, securing a 7–3 Alabama victory with a play forever known as "the Run in the Mud."

50 HIS "GREATEST TEAM EVER"

That's what Bear Bryant called his 1966 team—and it didn't win the national championship. The '66 team went 11–0, but both Notre Dame and Michigan State, which played an epic 10–10 tie that season, were voted ahead of the Crimson Tide. The season was capped with a 34–7 thrashing of Nebraska in the Sugar Bowl, and quarterback Ken Stabler was named the game's Most Valuable Player.

51 PRIME TIME

On October 4, 1969, Alabama faced Mississippi in one of the first prime-time telecasts of a college football game. It turned into the show of shows. Ole Miss quarterback Archie Manning was brilliant, completing 33 of 52 passes for 436 yards. He also ran for 104 yards, in a game that went back and forth from start to finish. But it was Alabama's Scott Hunter who won the night, completing 22 of 29 passes for 300 yards, including the game winner to George Ranager to give Alabama a 33–32 victory. Alabama had also been part of the first prime-time college football telecast, when the 1965 Orange Bowl against Texas was shown at night.

52 A WISH COMES TRUE

Among Bear Bryant's greatest attributes was his sense of the moment. He understood, after his football program saw a dip in success during the late 1960s and into 1970, that something needed to change. That change came during preseason practice before the 1971 season. Without telling the outside world, Bryant and his staff went to work rebuilding the Alabama offensive scheme, adopting the wishbone attack. It was a dramatic change for a program that had run a more traditional-style offense, but it had an immediate effect. At the opener, Southern California's Trojans weren't prepared for the new look of the Crimson Tide, which posted a 17–10 victory. It was the beginning of another golden age in Alabama football history.

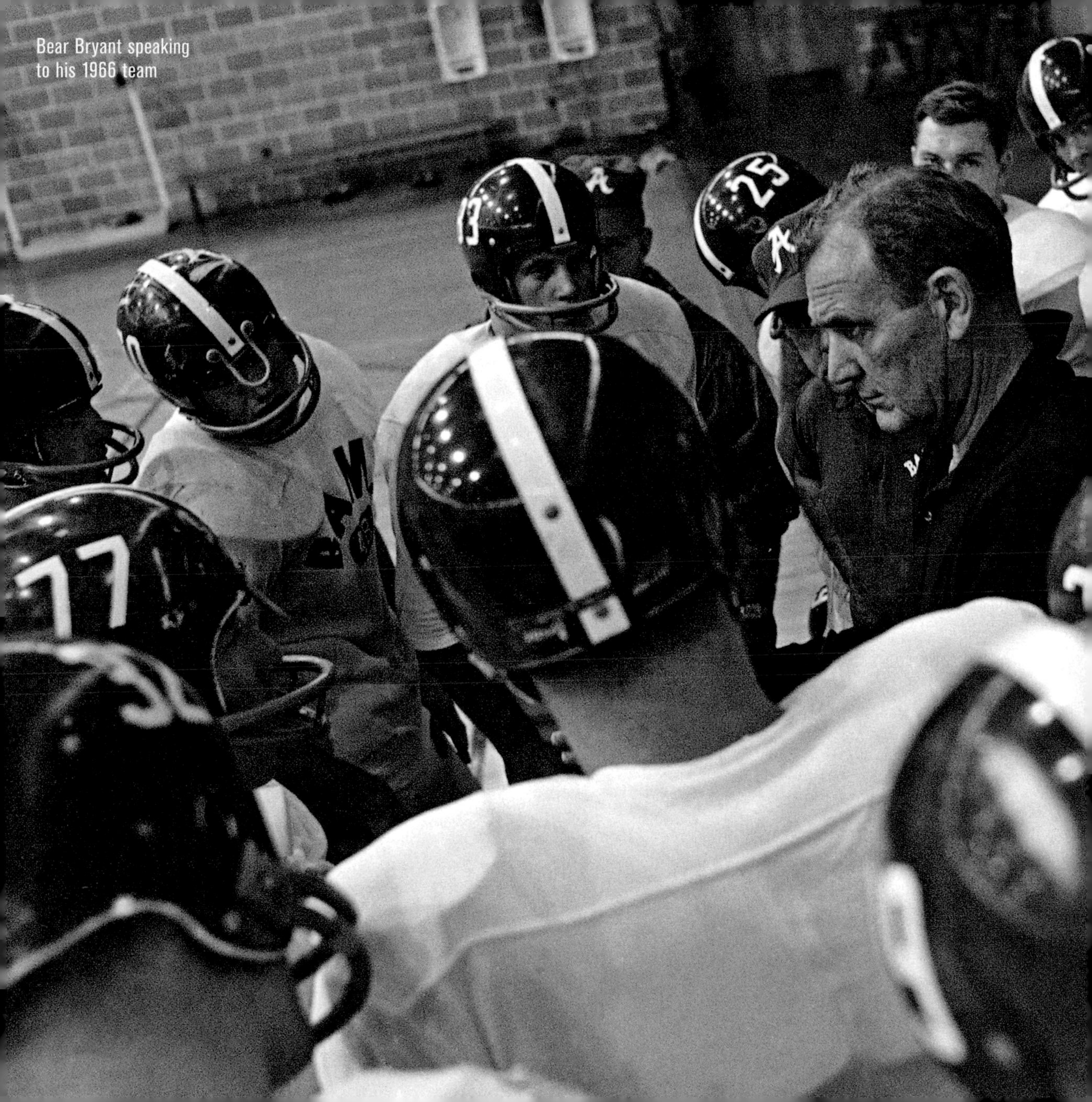

Bear Bryant speaking
to his 1966 team

53 THE ITALIAN STALLION

That's what Alabama fans came to call halfback Johnny Musso, who became one of the program's most beloved players for his relentless, pounding running style. Musso was a two-time All-American in 1970 and 1971, and he still ranks among Alabama's all-time leaders with 38 career touchdowns and 2,741 rushing yards. As a senior, Musso finished fourth in the Heisman Trophy voting but shared the SEC Player of the Year award with Heisman winner Pat Sullivan of Auburn.

54 TEARING AWAY

Bringing down Johnny Musso was tough enough because of his churning running style. It became nearly impossible for Auburn on November 28, 1970. That day, Musso rushed for 221 yards on 42 carries. Getting a grip on Musso wasn't enough. Musso wore special acid-dipped jerseys that tore away easily, making it even more difficult for defenders to bring him down. The Tigers' defense shredded eleven of Musso's jerseys.

Johnny Musso (22) cartwheels after being hit by Mississippi's Jim Poole, 1970.

Alabama's John Parker Wilson eludes
Tennessee's Turk McBride, 2006.

55 THE THIRD SATURDAY IN OCTOBER

Though not quite on the level of the Auburn rivalry, Alabama's annual date with Tennessee reaches beyond the realm of routine. The two schools began playing football against each other more than a century ago—their first meeting was a 6–6 tie in 1901—and it has always been among the most colorful showdowns in the Southeastern Conference. It helped that the fire was fueled for years by Tennessee coach Robert Neyland and Alabama's Bear Bryant. For years, the game was always played on the third Saturday in October, earning its nickname. In recent years, however, the game only occasionally falls on its traditional date. Through the 2008 season, Alabama holds the all-time lead in the series, 46–38–7.

56 WILBUR JACKSON

To measure Jackson's impact on the Alabama football program strictly by statistics would be impressive enough. Recruited as a wide receiver out of high school and converted to running back when Alabama unveiled its wishbone offense in the 1970s, Jackson was All-SEC and All-American in 1973, when he averaged 7.9 yards per carry. But he also owns the distinction of being the first African-American football signee at Alabama. Jackson would later play in the NFL, where he was a member of the Washington Redskins' 1982 Super Bowl championship team.

"I don't have any black players. I don't have any white players, either. I only have football players."

—Bear Bryant

John Hannah

57 CAN'T LOSE IN BATON ROUGE

For all the history and reputation surrounding LSU's Memorial Stadium, it proved to be one of Alabama's favorite places to spend a football Saturday for nearly three decades. Starting in 1971, Alabama did not lose in Baton Rouge until the year 2000, a staggering stretch of 15 games against one of the strongest programs in college football year in and year out. There was one season—1985—when Alabama and LSU tied, 14–14; otherwise, Baton Rouge became a home away from home for the Crimson Tide.

58 JOHN HANNAH

In 1981, *Sports Illustrated* magazine proclaimed on its cover that John Hannah was the "best offensive lineman of all time." And he may be. Hannah played three years at guard and tackle for Bear Bryant's Alabama teams, from 1970 through 1972. He was a two-time All-American and was named to Alabama's All-Century team. However, it was in the NFL, where Hannah played for the New England Patriots, that he became a defining force. Whether it was pass blocking, pulling on a sweep, or just doing the dirty work on a play up the middle, Hannah came to symbolize offensive line play at its best.

"John Hannah is the best offensive lineman I ever coached."

—Bear Bryant

59 TUSCALOOSA

It's home to the University of Alabama and has its own unique charms. Located in west-central Alabama on the banks of the Black Warrior River, Tuscaloosa is more than a college town, though there are about 27,000 students enrolled in the town of roughly 83,000 residents. From 1826 through 1846, Tuscaloosa was the capital of Alabama, and during that time—in 1831—the University of Alabama was established. The capital eventually moved to Montgomery, but the university stayed, and Tuscaloosa has grown around it. In the world of college football, when people mention Tuscaloosa, everybody knows what they're talking about.

60 THE PRESIDENT'S MANSION

The stately white home that sits just off University Boulevard and not far from Bryant-Denny Stadium is among the treasures of the school's campus. Built between 1839 and 1841, the house was first occupied by President Basil Manly in 1841. However, it was in 1865 that the house became an enduring symbol not just of the university but of the entire state. As the story goes, when Union troops were destroying the Alabama campus, Louisa Frances Garland, the wife of school president Landon C. Garland, saved the house, one of the few structures that survived the Civil War.

61 OZZIE NEWSOME

He came to be called "the Wizard of Oz," and for good reason. Few players have ever been better at their position than Ozzie Newsome. At Alabama, Newsome was a four-year starter at split end, and with a tough, muscular style, he became one of the dominant players of the 1970s. With Newsome playing a key role, Alabama posted a 42–6 record during his career, which included 102 receptions. Newsome's star grew even brighter after college. He was a three-time Pro Bowl player for the Cleveland Browns, where he ended his career with 662 receptions and 47 touchdowns. He is now the general manager of the NFL's Baltimore Ravens.

"*Martin Luther King, Jr., preached equality. Coach Bryant practiced it.*"

—Ozzie Newsome

62 BEAR VERSUS WOODY

The iconic coaching matchup came in the 1978 Sugar Bowl, which pitted the Crimson Tide against Woody Hayes' Ohio State Buckeyes. Although it paired two of college football's legendary coaches and characters, it wasn't much of a game. Alabama hammered Ohio State, 35–6, in a game that was as one-sided as the score indicated. There was plenty of grumbling from the Buckeyes' side, in part because they were accustomed to playing in the Rose Bowl and New Orleans wasn't Pasadena. It didn't help that Ohio State spent two weeks in New Orleans preparing for the game, a scheduling mistake that siphoned the enthusiasm from the Buckeyes. Alabama arrived fresh, won easily, and thought it might be awarded the national championship. Instead, that honor went to Notre Dame.

63 THE 1978 TEAM

To say the Crimson Tide posted an 11–1 record and beat top-ranked Penn State in one of the most memorable Sugar Bowls ever doesn't do justice to what happened in 1978. Led by All-Americans Barry Krauss and Marty Lyons, the Crimson Tide played a ferocious schedule that included games against Nebraska, Missouri, Southern Cal, Washington, Florida, Tennessee, LSU, and Auburn. The Tide's only loss was a 24–14 decision to Southern Cal early in the year. Otherwise, the succession of impressive victories culminated in New Orleans with the victory over Penn State that earned Alabama its 10th national championship.

64 THE STAND

It came down to a simple moment: Near the end of the 1979 Sugar Bowl, Penn State, boasting a 19-game winning streak, faced fourth-and-goal from inside the Alabama 1-yard line. Trailing, 14–7, the Nittany Lions needed a touchdown and extra point to tie the game and perhaps claim the national championship. The play was a basic dive into the line by Penn State's Mike Guman, but it was blown up by Alabama linebacker Barry Krauss. With the Superdome crowd roaring, Guman took a handoff; as he approached the goal line, intending to leap over it, Krauss came soaring in, stopping Guman instantly to win the game for the Crimson Tide. Legendary college football voice Keith Jackson set the scene for the national television audience, and when the play began, Jackson said, "Fusina hands to Guman. He didn't make it! He didn't make it! What an unbelievable goal-line stand by Alabama!" Decades later, it remains one of the defining moments in Alabama football history.

Penn State's Mike Guman (24) is stopped by Barry Krauss (77), along with Murray Legg (19) and Rich Wingo (36).

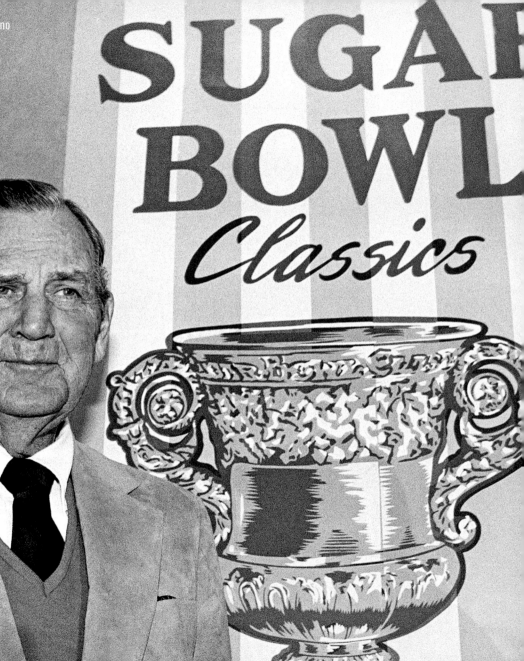

Bear Bryant and Joe Paterno

65 BEAR VERSUS JoePa

When top-ranked Penn State faced No. 2 Alabama in the 1979 Sugar Bowl, it was only the fifth time the two top-ranked teams in college football had met in a bowl game. As big as the game was, the coaches were almost bigger. In Joe Paterno's case, it was a chance for Penn State to win the elusive national championship. In the television intro to the game, Paterno said, "This is the biggest football game Penn State has ever played.... We'd really like to get one [national championship]."

Of course, the Crimson Tide won that night, and Bear Bryant had a 4–0 career record against the Nittany Lions. Nineteen years after Bryant retired as college football's winningest Division I coach in 1982, Paterno finally beat Bryant, passing him on the all-time victory list.

"Even his peers in the coaching business felt in awe of him. He had such charisma. Whatever it is that makes great generals, he had it. Tons of it."

–Joe Paterno on Bear Bryant in the book *Coach: The Life of Paul Bear Bryant*

Don McNeal (28, inset) intercepts a pass intended for Penn State's Bob Bassett (81). Alabama's Jim Bob Harris (9) is also in on the play.

66 THE 28-GAME WINNING STREAK

When the Crimson Tide lost to Southern Cal early in the 1978 season, it was a disappointment, but no one imagined it would be more than two years before Alabama would lose another football game. The Tide closed out the 1978 season with nine consecutive victories and kept going in 1979, rolling to a 12–0 record and its second straight national championship. When 1980 arrived, Alabama was chasing more than a third consecutive national championship. It was chasing Oklahoma's all-time record of 47 consecutive victories. The Tide didn't get that far, but it did stretch its winning streak to 28 games before a 6–3 loss to Mississippi State put an end to the ride. Still, it left Alabama with the 15th-longest winning streak in college football history.

67 DON McNEAL

For a man who didn't play football until his junior year in high school, McNeal had a spectacular career. He was a defensive back for the Crimson Tide from 1977 through 1979, making him a part of two national championship teams and eventually earning him a place on Alabama's All-Centennial Team. While the fame belonged to Barry Krauss for his national championship–saving stop against Penn State in the famous Sugar Bowl goal-line stand, it was McNeal who had a touchdown-saving stop on second down that set up the dramatic finish. After Alabama, McNeal spent nine years playing for the Miami Dolphins.

Dwight Stephenson (57) snaps the ball to Jeff Rutledge, 1979.

68 THE 1979 TEAM

It was the perfect way to end a remarkable decade in Alabama football. Coming off a national championship in 1978, the Crimson Tide dominated the college football landscape in 1979. Stocked with talent that included center Dwight Stephenson and loaded with confidence, Alabama rolled to a 12–0 record. In the season's first five weeks, Alabama showed its superiority by outscoring its opponents 219–9. Over the course of the season, the Crimson Tide allowed only 67 points and capped the year with a 24–9 victory over Arkansas in the Sugar Bowl.

69 DWIGHT STEPHENSON

A quiet man, Stephenson had a thunderous impact. He is regarded as one of the best ever to play center at any level, and Bear Bryant called Stephenson the best player he ever coached. That's how good he was. At Alabama, Stephenson was three-time All-SEC performer from 1977 through 1979 and part of a 21-game Crimson Tide winning streak. In the NFL, Stephenson's reputation grew, eventually earning him a spot in the Pro Football Hall of Fame. Just as impressively, Stephenson was awarded the NFL's prestigious Walter Payton Man of the Year award in 1985.

"If I could tell a young player to learn from one of my veterans, to follow around and copy one player, that player would always be Dwight."

–Former Miami Dolphins coach Don Shula

70 THE 1982 LIBERTY BOWL

Exactly two weeks before a 7–4 Alabama team was scheduled to meet Illinois in the Liberty Bowl in Memphis, Bear Bryant shocked college football by announcing that he would retire after the game. Suddenly, the game became an enormous moment. Although Bryant tried to downplay his role, it was impossible. There was a story-book quality to Alabama's 21–15 victory over the Illini on December 29, 1982. In Bryant's last game, the Crimson Tide got a 1-yard touchdown run from Craig Turner in the fourth quarter to give Bryant his 323rd and final coaching victory. Bryant was quoted afterward as saying, "We won in spite of me." In fact, the Crimson Tide won because of him.

Bear Bryant is carried off the field following his team's victory over Illinois in the 1982 Liberty Bowl.

71 REMEMBERING BEAR BRYANT

When the news hit on the afternoon of January 26, 1983, that Bear Bryant had died, it rippled across the country. The three network broadcasts led that evening with the news that four weeks after coaching his final game, Bryant had passed away from heart failure while in a hospital room. Just hours before, Bryant had met with his successor, Ray Perkins, to talk about the future of the program. On January 28, mourners lined the 55-mile route from Tuscaloosa to Birmingham as Bryant's body was taken to its final resting place at Elmwood Cemetery in Birmingham. Eight of Bryant's former players served as pallbearers, as a sport and the country remembered the coach.

72 RAY PERKINS

Being the football coach who succeeded Bear Bryant would not have been easy for anyone, and it wasn't for Ray Perkins. He had played under Bryant during a glorious run in the mid-1960s when the Tide won three consecutive SEC titles from 1964 to 1966, twice capping the seasons with national championships. As Bryant's successor, not necessarily the one everyone wanted, Perkins faced enormous pressure and expectations. He spent four seasons as the Crimson Tide's head coach, building a 32–15–1 record that included three bowl games and one losing season. After four years, Perkins had enough and left to coach in the NFL.

"The greatest honor of my life is following that man.... I'm not replacing him; I'm following him."

—Ray Perkins in *Sports Illustrated*

Ray Perkins signing autographs
for young fans, 1966

73 MARTY LYONS

He was big, fast, and strong and had a knack for being in the right place at the right time, not just during his Alabama career but in his 11 seasons with the NFL's New York Jets. Lyons was an All-American defensive tackle who had 202 career tackles, six forced fumbles, and four recoveries. During the Crimson Tide's famous goal-line stand against Penn State in the Sugar Bowl, the Nittany Lions faced fourth down from inside the Alabama 1-yard line. As Penn State approached the line, Lyons barked, "You'd better pass," to Penn State quarterback Chuck Fusina. Instead, the Nittany Lions' running play failed, as Lyons had suggested it would. Lyons went on to become part of the Jets' famous "New York Sack Exchange" defensive line.

Left: Marty Lyons
Right: Van Tiffin kicks as Larry Abney holds.

74 VAN TIFFIN'S KICK

Six seconds remained in the 1985 Iron Bowl and Auburn led Alabama, 23–22, when Crimson Tide kicker Van Tiffin trotted onto the field. Tiffin had already kicked field goals of 26, 32, and 42 yards while missing a 52-yarder in the game. None of that mattered anymore. It all came down to one kick into a slight breeze in the November darkness. Tiffin, who set a school record with a 57-yard field goal against Texas A&M in 1985 and made a school-record 135 consecutive extra points, had the chance to earn a place in Alabama history with one kick. And he took it.

"He made it!" ABC announcer Keith Jackson shouted as the kick sailed through the uprights and time expired. It may never be forgotten.

"Playing at Alabama taught me mental toughness, being a team player, and being a winner."
–Cornelius Bennett

75 CORNELIUS BENNETT

As a linebacker at Alabama and then later in the NFL, Bennett was like an unstoppable force of nature. He didn't just play football. He imposed himself on the game, particularly on opponents. As a senior in 1986, Bennett was good enough that, despite being a defensive player, he finished seventh in the Heisman Trophy balloting. Bennett was the SEC's Player of the Year in 1986 and won the Lombardi Award to cap a career that eventually earned him a spot in the College Football Hall of Fame. In the NFL, Bennett continued to have a forceful impact, playing in five Super Bowls (though he never played on the winning team).

76 THE SACK

In a 1986 game against Notre Dame, Alabama's Cornelius Bennett delivered a hit that still resonates more than 30 years later. The Fighting Irish had the ball near their own 30-yard line when quarterback Steve Beuerlein took the snap. Beuerlein faked a handoff as he dropped back to pass—and that is all he remembers. Coming off the left end like a hurricane, Bennett—who was nicknamed "Biscuit" because of his fondness for his mother's biscuits—had an unimpeded shot at the Notre Dame quarterback. Before Beuerlein could react, Bennett launched himself into the quarterback, literally knocking him off his feet and backward. And unconscious. The play resulted in an Alabama fumble recovery and a perpetual place in the loop of memorable quarterback sacks.

"I just want to thank God for blessing me with some athletic talent and letting me play for the University of Alabama."

–Derrick Thomas

77 BOBBY HUMPHREY

Over the course of his Alabama career, Humphrey always found a way to produce. A two-time All-American, Humphrey's name pops up throughout the Alabama record book. Through 2008, he still owns the program's single-season rushing record (1,471 in 1986) and is the second all-time leading rusher (3,420 yards). He owns two of the five best rushing seasons in school history and had four 200-yard games in his career. The finest may have been in Humphrey's senior year, when he gained 220 yards against Penn State. At one stretch in the game, Humphrey carried the ball 12 straight times for the Crimson Tide.

78 DERRICK THOMAS

Thomas was a furious and, at times, seemingly unstoppable force as a linebacker. Blessed with an extraordinary blend of speed, size, and football instincts, Thomas terrorized opponents like few others. In his senior year at Alabama, the All-American linebacker was credited with 27 quarterback sacks and placed among the top 10 in Heisman Trophy balloting. As a pro, Thomas had an exceptional career, defining his position during the 1990s, when he was a nine-time All-Pro player for the Kansas City Chiefs. He had 126.5 career sacks, including an NFL-record seven sacks in a game against Seattle. Thomas' career ended suddenly when he was involved in an auto accident on January 23, 2000, and died two weeks later. He was elected into the Pro Football Hall of Fame in 2009.

Gene Stallings celebrating Alabama's
victory in the 1993 Sugar Bowl
Inset: Gene and John Mark Stallings

79 GENE STALLINGS

He had a coaching pedigree few could match—Stallings served as an assistant coach to Bear Bryant at Alabama and to Tom Landry with the Dallas Cowboys. That's what convinced Alabama officials that Stallings was the right man to lead the program when they hired him in 1990. Stallings had spent seven years in Tuscaloosa with Bryant before his career took him to Texas A&M, the Cowboys, and the St. Louis/Phoenix Cardinals. At Alabama from 1990 through 1996, Stallings coached the Tide to the 1992 national championship with a defense recognized as one of the best in SEC history.

80 JOHN MARK STALLINGS

Perhaps Alabama athletic director Mal Moore said it best when the 46-year-old son of Gene Stallings passed away in August 2008: "For someone who never played or coached a game, I think John Mark may have touched more Alabama fans than any other person ever did." John Mark Stallings was born with Down syndrome, but he became a fixture around the program. In an effort to help others, Gene Stallings and his family played a major role in developing the Rise School in Tuscaloosa, a place where young children with disabilities could get help. In memory of John Mark Stallings, the Alabama football program named the team's equipment room after him.

George Teague (13) stops Louisiana Tech running back.

81 GEORGE TEAGUE

An offside penalty may have nullified the most memorable play in George Teague's Alabama football career, but that couldn't dull its shine. In the 1993 Sugar Bowl against Miami, with the national championship on the line, Teague—a safety—had helped stake the Tide to a big lead with a 31-yard interception return for a touchdown. Later, Miami receiver Lamar Thomas appeared headed to a long touchdown reception when, seemingly out of nowhere, Teague chased him down from behind. In a continuous motion, Teague stripped the ball from Thomas, then returned the ball upfield in a play Tide fans still call "The Strip." Teague is also remembered as the Dallas Cowboys player who flattened San Francisco's Terrell Owens in 2000, when the flamboyant wide receiver celebrated a touchdown pass on the famous star in Texas Stadium.

82 THE DEUCE

David Palmer stood 5 feet 9 inches tall, weighed 170 pounds, and was so much bigger than that. Nicknamed "the Deuce" because he wore No. 2, Palmer played football with an electrifying style. In 1993, Palmer became the first Alabama player to have 1,000 receiving yards in one season, but he did much more. When Palmer waited to return a punt, the stadium waited with him, knowing he was capable of magic. Palmer was good enough as a junior that he finished third in the Heisman Trophy voting, the highest ever for a Crimson Tide player. He bypassed his senior year and spent seven seasons in the NFL playing for the Minnesota Vikings.

"Every time I touch the ball, I think I can score."

—David Palmer in the *New York Times*

83 THE 1992 TEAM

In the 100th season of Alabama football, the Crimson Tide celebrated with another national championship. It was coach Gene Stallings' third Alabama team, and it was a classic. Led by quarterback Jay Barker and a stingy defense, the Crimson Tide methodically plowed through its regular-season schedule and then beat Florida in the SEC championship. All that was left was a matchup with mighty Miami, ranked No. 1 and featuring Heisman Trophy–winning quarterback Gino Torretta in the Sugar Bowl. What was expected to be a titanic struggle instead became a coronation for the Crimson Tide, which rolled to a 34–13 victory to claim its first national title since 1979.

ALABAMA CRIMSON TIDE

ALABAMA CRIMSON TIDE.

Sherman Williams (20) scores in the 1993 Sugar Bowl.

84 JAY BARKER

You've heard the expression a thousand times: A coach or a recruiting expert looks at a player and says, "He's a winner." In most cases, it's just another platitude. In Jay Barker's case, it's a spot-on definition. Barker played quarterback for three seasons at Alabama, leading the Crimson Tide to the 1992 national championship, winning the 1994 Johnny Unitas Golden Arm Award, and finishing fifth in the Heisman Trophy race. When Barker left Alabama for a seven-year professional football career, he was a winner. His career record of 35–2–1 is the best ever among Crimson Tide quarterbacks.

85 THE HEISMAN TROPHY

It would seem natural that college football's highest individual award would have found a home in one of the sport's most successful programs. But no Alabama player has ever won the Heisman Trophy. That doesn't mean the Crimson Tide hasn't produced exceptional players. In fact, 16 different Alabama players have finished among the top 10 in Heisman Trophy voting, including David Palmer, who finished third in 1993.

86 "RUN, FORREST, RUN"

In the movie *Forrest Gump*, bullies are chasing Forrest when he takes off running one day. He keeps running and winds up tearing through a high school football game where Alabama coach Bear Bryant is scouting players. Curious about Gump's speed, Bryant recruits the young man and makes him a Crimson Tide running back. Gump becomes an All-American at Alabama, earning a chance to meet President John F. Kennedy in the White House. In the movie, of course.

"Now you wouldn't believe me if I told you, but I could run like the wind blows.... If I was ever going somewhere, I was running."

—Forrest Gump

Jay Barker

87 MAL MOORE

The university's board of trustees summed up Moore's contributions to the school when it renamed the Alabama football building as the Mal Moore Athletic Facility in 2007. Moore first arrived in Tuscaloosa in 1958, the same year Bear Bryant returned to coach the football program, and has since become an integral part of the Crimson Tide athletic legacy. Moore has been part of seven football national championships—one as a player and six as an assistant coach—and he has been the school's athletic director since 1999.

88 CHRIS SAMUELS

Glory does not come easily to offensive linemen. They do the hard work, the heavy lifting, the hidden magic. At Alabama, they have been some of the program's greatest football players. Like John Hannah, Dwight Stephenson, and others before him, Chris Samuels has a place along the Crimson Tide's all-time offensive line. Winner of the 1999 Outland Trophy as the nation's best offensive lineman, it was Samuels who cleared many of the holes for running back Shaun Alexander. Samuels was good enough to be the third overall pick in the 2000 NFL draft.

"My brothers helped me prepare for life in football by beating up on me all the time."

—Chris Samuels in *Sports Illustrated*

Chris Samuels

89 RAMMER JAMMER YELLOW HAMMER

It's a cheer that's as much a part of Alabama football as Dreamland ribs and crimson jerseys. It goes like this:

"Hey, Auburn!
Hey, Auburn!
Hey, Auburn!
We're gonna beat the hell outta you!
Rammer Jammer Yellow Hammer!
Give 'em hell, Alabama!"

One of the beauties of the verse is how easily any opponent's name can be substituted for Auburn's—and after the game, if the Tide has won, it can be updated to say, "We just beat the hell outta you."

90 RAMMER JAMMER, PART 2

In 2004, author Warren St. John released the book *Rammer Jammer Yellow Hammer: A Road Trip into the Heart of Fan Mania* and not only illuminated the fanatically devoted culture of Alabama football but also provided a wide-angle glimpse into the psyche of sports fans. Built around St. John's chronicling of a Crimson Tide football season, the book became a national best-seller with its blend of humor and insight. It was more than a sports book; it became a must-read. If you didn't understand Alabama football before, you did when you were done. If you already knew what the fuss was all about, you appreciated it even more.

Nikita Stover runs for a touchdown against Auburn, 2006.

"*I want to score every time I touch the ball.*"
—Shaun Alexander

Shaun Alexander dragging a Florida
defender into the end zone
Inset: Shaun Alexander

91 SHAUN ALEXANDER

Alexander came to Alabama after a remarkable high school career, carrying enormous expectations, and he delivered. Wearing No. 37, he became Alabama's all-time rushing leader with a style that combined speed, power, and a talent for shedding tacklers. Alexander's Alabama career included a string of memorable plays, including his 25-yard touchdown run to beat third-ranked Florida in overtime and a three-touchdown performance in a comeback victory over Auburn. As a senior, Alexander rushed for 1,383 yards scored and 24 touchdowns. In the NFL, Alexander spent eight legacy-sealing seasons with the Seattle Seahawks, where he was named the league's Most Valuable Player in 2005.

92 ALEXANDER THE GREAT

On November 9, 1996, in Baton Rouge, Louisiana, Shaun Alexander cemented his place among the legends of Alabama football. A freshman, Alexander set a school record by rushing for 291 yards on 20 carries, shredding the Tigers' defense and spoiling one of those famous Saturday nights in Tiger Stadium as the Crimson Tide rolled to a 26–0 victory. There was an almost elegant simplicity to the game's scoring. It went like this:

- 2nd quarter: Alexander, 17-yard touchdown run
- 3rd quarter: Alexander, 73-yard touchdown run
- 3rd quarter: Alexander, 72-yard touchdown run
- 4th quarter: Alexander, 12-yard touchdown run

Tyrone Prothro makes a miracle catch over
Southern Mississippi's Jasper Faulk, 2005.

93 TWICE AS NICE

In 1999, Alabama doubled its pleasure by beating Coach Steve Spurrier and the Florida Gators not once but twice in the same season. The first victory came in early October, when the Crimson Tide faced the third-ranked Gators in Gainesville, Florida. In an emotional back-and-forth game, Alabama won, 40–39, in overtime with a bizarre finish. In overtime, Florida scored a touchdown but missed the extra point. Alabama countered with its own touchdown, and a victory seemed certain—until the Crimson Tide also missed its extra point. A penalty allowed Alabama a second chance, and this time the extra point finished the Gators. More than two months later, the teams met again in the SEC championship game. Behind quarterbacks Andrew Zow and Tyler Watts, along with running back Shaun Alexander, Alabama blasted the Gators, 34–7, to complete a rare double.

94 THE CATCH

Twenty-nine seconds remained in the first half of Alabama's game against Southern Mississippi in 2005 when Crimson Tide quarterback Brodie Croyle dropped back on fourth down to pass and wide receiver Tyrone Prothro went deep down the middle. While the Bryant-Denny Stadium crowd watched, Prothro and Southern Miss defensive back Jasper Faulk ran stride for stride toward the end zone as Croyle's pass came down. What happened next was remarkable. Looking back for the ball, Prothro managed to reach behind Faulk and grab it—catching it on Faulk's back—before tumbling to the ground with the reception near the goal line. It remains one of the most spectacular receptions in college football history.

Fans jam Bryant-Denny Stadium for 2007 A-Day.

95 A-DAY

At some places, it's called the spring game. At Alabama, it's A-Day, and it's so much more than an intrasquad scrimmage at the end of spring practice. It's an all-day on-campus celebration in April, culminating with a look at the football team almost five months before the season begins. And it's like nowhere else. In 2007, a crowd of 92,138 fans attended the spring game, an all-time college football record. In 2008, the attendance was 78,200. It's called passion.

96 THE COACHING CLINIC

The art and science of football is the centerpiece of Alabama's annual springtime coaching clinic, which brings football coaches from across the country to study and share concepts about the game. Typically held during spring practice, the clinic is an opportunity for coaches to network, listen to lectures, and watch the Crimson Tide up close during off-season workouts. There's nothing small time about it. The 2008 coaching clinic included talks from New England Patriots coach Bill Belichick, former Georgia coach Vince Dooley, and Virginia coach Al Groh, among others, including members of Nick Saban's Alabama staff.

97 NICK SABAN

The 27th football coach in Alabama history, Saban arrived in 2007 intent on restoring the program to its place atop the college football kingdom. Known for his intensity, organization, and devotion, Saban immediately recharged the program. Saban is more than a football coach. With his agreement to an eight-year, $32 million contract that was the richest ever for a college football coach, Saban accepted total control of the Alabama football program. He believes in discipline, personal responsibility, and commitment. Saban is not without controversy, especially after he left the NFL's Miami Dolphins to accept the Alabama job. When Saban's plane landed in Tuscaloosa on the day he was to be introduced as the new football coach, more than a thousand people were there to greet him.

98 RETURN TO GLORY

In 2007, Nick Saban's first season at Alabama, the Crimson Tide posted a 7–6 record. It was modest by Alabama standards, but encouraging because it was only the second winning season in five years. By 2008, it began to feel like old times again. Starting the season with a dominating 34–10 victory over ninth-ranked Clemson in the season opener in Atlanta, the Crimson Tide became the story of college football's regular season. The team won at Georgia, it won at Tennessee, and in an emotional return for Saban to LSU, where he formerly coached, the Tide won in overtime. It was an 11–0 regular season capped by a 36–0 victory over Auburn. Although Alabama lost to Florida in the SEC championship game and later to Utah in the Sugar Bowl, the glory days had returned.

Nick Saban leads the Crimson Tide onto the field.

Teammates congratulating Sherman Williams (20)
after he scored in the 1993 Sugar Bowl

99 GOING BOWLING

Bowl games come naturally to Alabama. In fact, the Crimson Tide has played in more bowl games (56) than any other program. Alabama has a 31–22–3 record in bowl games since making its first appearance in the 1926 Rose Bowl, a game the Tide won, 20–19, against Washington. The Sugar Bowl has been Alabama's most familiar postseason destination: The Tide has played 13 times in the New Orleans game, winning eight times.

100 THE SEC CHAMPIONSHIPS

There have been 25 of them, four in the Southern Conference, then an amazing 21 in the Southeastern Conference. Alabama's football prowess began to show itself when it won four Southern Conference titles in seven years: 1924, 1925, 1926, and 1930. When the Tide left to join the new SEC, the dominance continued. Alabama's 21 SEC championships are easily the most in league history. The most impressive run began in 1971, when Alabama won the first of what would be nine SEC championships in 11 years. Like children, though, each of them is special.

The years: 1924, 1925, 1926, 1930, 1933, 1934, 1937, 1945, 1953, 1961, 1964, 1965, 1966, 1971, 1972, 1973, 1974, 1975, 1977, 1978, 1979, 1981, 1989, 1992, 1999

John Parker Wilson (14) and Baron Huber (40) celebrate Wilson's 1-yard touchdown run versus Tennessee, 2008.

Coach Bryant is carried off the field by his players following a 34–7 rout of Nebraska in the 1967 Sugar Bowl.

101 THE NATIONAL CHAMPIONSHIPS

There are eight consensus national championships in Alabama's football history. There are four other seasons (1930, 1934, 1941, and 1973) in which Alabama can claim at least a share of the national championship. They have come in six different decades with four different coaches—Wallace Wade, Frank Thomas, Bear Bryant, and Gene Stallings. They have come with offense, with defense, and with the rare passion that defines Alabama football.

The consensus national championship years: 1925, 1926, 1961, 1964, 1965, 1978, 1979, 1992

ACKNOWLEDGMENTS

This begins with a special thank you to Ann Stratton and Leslie Stoker and the other fine people at Stewart, Tabori & Chang, where they produce books that enlighten, inform, and entertain us.

Also, a special thanks to Mary Tiegreen, whose vision has led to the creation of this book and others like it. She understands the passion that ties together the people, the places, and the games they play.

Thanks to Taylor Zarzour and Mike Gordon, whose Alabama bloodlines helped me see and feel what they do when the subject is Crimson Tide football.

Again, thanks to my brother, Dave, who brought this all together and excels in the magic of creating art.

To copy editor Richard Slovak, Ted Ciuzio of AP Images, Tim Williams of Collegiate Images, and the people at the Paul W. Bryant Museum, your time and efforts are greatly appreciated.

To my wife, Tamera, and my daughter, Molly; my parents, Ron and Beth Green; and my extended family, whose allegiances cross conference boundaries in a variety of directions, there aren't enough thanks.

And finally, to the people who believe that Alabama football is something special, your passion defines you. Roll Tide.

Left: Ken Stabler (12) versus Tennessee, circa 1966

A Tiegreen Book

Published in 2009 by Stewart, Tabori & Chang
An imprint of ABRAMS

All rights reserved. No portion of this book may be repro-
duced, stored in a retrieval system, or transmitted in any
form or by any means, mechanical, electronic, photocopying,
recording, or otherwise, without written permission from the
publisher.

Stewart, Tabori & Chang books are available at special dis-
counts when purchased in quantity for premiums and promo-
tions as well as fundraising or educational use. Special editions
can also be created to specification. For details, contact
specialmarkets@hnabooks.com.

Library of Congress Cataloging-in-Publication Data

Green, Ron, 1956-
    101 reasons to love Alabama football / Ron Green, Jr.
        p. cm.
    Includes bibliographical references and index.
    ISBN 978-1-58479-810-1 (alk. paper)
    1. University of Alabama--Football--History. 2. Alabama
Crimson Tide
(Football team)--History. I. Title. II. Title: One hundred one
reasons to
love Alabama football. III. Title: One hundred and one reasons
to love
Alabama football.
    GV958.A4G74 2009
    796.332'630976184--dc22

                                    2009012575

Text copyright © 2009 Ron Green, Jr.
Compilation copyright © 2009 Mary Tiegreen

Editor: Ann Stratton
Designer: David Green, Brightgreen Design
Production Manager: Tina Cameron

101 Reasons to Love Alabama Football is a book in the 101
REASONS TO LOVE™ series.

101 REASONS TO LOVE™ is a trademark of
Mary Tiegreen and Hubert Pedroli.

Printed and bound in China
10 9 8 7 6 5 4 3 2 1

ABRAMS
THE ART OF BOOKS SINCE 1949
115 West 18th Street
New York, NY 10011
www.abramsbooks.com

Photo Credits

Alabama/ Collegiate Images: pages 1, 4–5, 8–9, 10–11, 12–13, 15, 16, 18, 19 (inset), 22 (inset),
23, 26, 27 (inset), 40 (inset), 41, 42–43, 47, 48 (hat), 56 (inset), 57, 58, 66, 69, 79 (inset), 81,
86, 88, 90, 92, 94, 99, 101, 104, 105 (inset), 106, 111, 118, 120

AP Images: pages 2–3, 6–7, 20, 21 (inset), 25, 28 (inset), 29, 30, 32, 34, 37, 38–39, 44, 45
(inset), 49, 50, 52, 54, 61, 62 (inset), 63, 64, 70–71, 72–73, 74, 76, 78, 82–83, 85, 87, 93 (inset),
97, 103, 108, 112–113, 114–115, 116–117

David Green: pages 96 (pennant)